I0756020

FINISHING LINE PRESS
www.finishinglinepress.com

City of Silver and Gold

poems by

Miles Liss

Finishing Line Press
Georgetown, Kentucky

City of Silver and Gold

ISBN 979-8-89990-374-8 First Edition

ACKNOWLEDGMENTS

I would like to thank my wife, the poet and writer Zakia Ahmadzai, who carefully read and labored over these poems, providing invaluable feedback, and my mother, Bonnie Liss-Holmberg, who provided her beautiful artwork for the cover. I would also like to thank my professors from Vermont College of Fine Arts, Richard Jackson, Betsy Sholl, and David Wojahn, for their support and feedback, the poet Yehoshua November for his support and kind words, and my cohorts in Yetzirah 2024, who encouraged me when I expressed doubt about this project. Finally, I would like to thank all the people at Finishing Line Press, including the publisher Leah Huete de Maines, who originally accepted this chapbook, and my editor, Christen Kincaid, who walked me through the publication process. This book is dedicated to all victims of war.

Publisher: Leah Huete de Maines
Editor: Christen Kincaid
Cover Art: Bonnie Liss
Author Photo: Zakia Ahmadzai
Cover Design: Elizabeth Maines McCleavy

Order online: www.finishinglinepress.com
also available on amazon.com

Author inquiries and mail orders:
Finishing Line Press
PO Box 1626
Georgetown, Kentucky 40324
USA

Contents

The Dollhouse Makers (October 7th Massacre)

When all the dollhouses you
so carefully constructed begin
to falter and to fold,

the mother and father grown
old or died, the baby's crib
overturned, the baby fully grown,

the wife who left and never returned,
the husband middle-aged, weighed
down with regret,

when the dollhouse itself, once a fixture
in some happy family's home, is lost
or given away at some yard sale,

then outside, yes, the sky is truly falling,
just as the weatherman predicted.

The ocean tides rise,
threatening to swallow the once
shining, imperial cities on the shore.

The helicopters twirl their blades
in an ever-blossoming war.

The pieces are broken.
The furniture's missing.
The kitchen and living room are in shambles.

Gone are the lampposts and telephone wires.
The jet planes and the cars. All swept away
by a monsoon that shoots lightning bolts

from its underbelly. The innocent
and the guilty, the sane and insane,
all are rocked to the core.

The dollhouses float away down
a ravenous rush of water and debris.

A sort of scrounging around for
whatever's left on this timid planet.

Ouroboros

I have two bullets.
One for the world
and one for me.

No matter how many times
I load my gun, it's always
the second one that fires.

How cold is the world.
Like a prisoner's cell.

Those who live in glass
houses and sip gin
cocktails have no idea.

The faces one sees.
The ignorant glances
lacking all humanity.

A puppy chases
its own tail, going
round and round.

In circles, my life seems.

Spinning circles that never
reach their end, like history
repeating itself.

Conflict in the Holy Land

The song rises but can't be heard.
Swirls in a painting refuse to take form.

The sag of flowers in the vase is final.
Nothing appears to grow here anymore.

Eyes are glazed over with smoke and fire.
A mother cries because her baby just won't feed.

Something burns between your teeth.
A piece of flesh that keeps your face from smiling.

You try to give your love away, but nobody wants it.
They refuse to acknowledge its existence.

We're dancing in the desert with old bones.
Dancing with the dead, who can no longer hear us.

Hold them close, see if you can make out
what they have to say.

Thousands of stars
in their empty sockets.

War Campaign

Sleep without reason
and reason without sleep.

The bells ring.
The fortress has been overthrown.

Men have lost their reason
once again.

Cigarettes and ashtrays,
letters torn up and unreceived.

We were a one man army.
In sacred unity we cried.

There's blood in the water
and the water is ours.

One cannot control
the uncontrollable.

One cannot remark
without being remarked upon.

The sky's a gray reminiscence
of all that was once holy.

The sea's a confusion
that drives deep into this century.

Song of the Child Victims

We are getting closer to knowing
what animals feel like
when they're slaughtered.

A cold snow and then
the hatchet or the gun.

We are lowing madly
before being hit
by their hammers.

Enemies in vibrant sparkling skins
and round eyes like robins
gaze at us ecstatically while we die.

You who created fate—
won't you listen to our cries?

We are the dying children
who cannot remember
our mothers' or fathers' faces.

They only dance before us
waving their hands—
headless strangers who fall

before
completing
their gyrations.

My Brother's Keeper

My brother in his army uniform
fell in the middle of the night
while a high wind was blowing.

His body dropped, a bullet to the head.
It sapped the electricity from his eyes.

They went blank, then they stared
at the red dirt and rocks of the desert.

We should have been wanderers
and moneylenders, given the space
to live by the grace and generosity

of foreign nations. Graceful as they
tell us where to live. Generous
in allowing us to breathe.

My brother lies dead in the sand.
He must be a skeleton by now.

The desert must have taken his bones.
Nothing left but a freshly pressed
uniform now faded and torn.

Will There Ever Be Peace?

Four years old and we
played in bomb shelters.
Fighter jets patrolled the sky.

David slew Goliath
in this land, but the
conflict continues.

At the funeral procession
of our prime minister
a convoy of tanks.

Generational Trauma as Viewed through a Gin and Tonic

Depression arrives with the first
rocket barrage. With the second,
loss of hope. The third, alienation.

And so on. But why speak
of such things? They're old hat.
Anyone who suffers will tell you—

the pickle won't fit in the pickle jar.
Strangers eyes are made of glass.
No one is who they appear to be.

This is the time for ice and refreshments.
You sip them slowly and try to ignore
the body count.

The protesters spray paint obscenities.
The sidewalks are filled with calls
for the death of your people.

The Half-Life of Hate

The web is broken.
The strands flap in the wind
back and forth like a dangling blanket.

People are frightened. They reach
out to each other. This day must be
a bad dream.

Years later it will debated whether
this was a liberation movement
or a tribal bloodletting.

The lifeless bodies rise above
a country now at war. They plead
for understanding in between bullets.

There is a rage here that will never
be washed away. A fire that threatens
to destroy the barn and its horses.

They neigh terribly,
raise their hoofs and kick.
One can read an animal fear in their eyes.

Others try to pull them away
from a conflagration that threatens
to be everlasting.

Memories of Once a Village

I remember camping out with Gili
beneath the constellations.
He must be a scientist now
if he's not dead. Such a bright
intelligence burned within him.

Simone, in her gown of tin foil stars.
She played Queen Esther on the stage.
Her hair looked like golden wheat shafts
touched by sun. Eyes bright, like a basket
of almonds at the shuk. Her mother took
her away one day on a boat that sailed
across the ocean to Australia.

And what of Deni the fisherman
who was left behind? How many fish
did he catch today? Can fish ever swim
in such turbulent waters or do their
silver bodies simply float on their sides
eyes staring blankly at the sky?

The Seagulls and the Whales

White seagulls surround the whales
and hurl invective. They rise and fall
over the swimming behemoths.

The mind's a terrorist, the way
it pokes and prods, searching
out its victims.

A pair of legs spread out
amidst a pool of blood.
The mind tastes its own suffering.

The rubble finds bodies
indiscriminate and unaware.
War's as inevitable as the fate on one's palm.

They cry out for justice, the seagulls,
in flocks that grow each day.
They screech and rip

another strip of flesh
from the whales, force
them to burrow underwater.

Leviathan

My brain is empty
scouring dreams that have lost
their way amidst knives and hand grenades.

I run through broken fields of corn.
I communicate with the dead.
Every night I speak with them
deep into the morning hours.

A jeep overturned, hit by an IED
leaves its driver legless.
The road is lined with landmines.

War is hell, they say. The generals
know this axiom all too well.
Patrols and rocket flares, each side
fighting for the land they love.

My thoughts have become lethal
and refuse to recede. When anger
and self-pity consume the mind, the mind
becomes a sea serpent of biblical proportions.

Call it what you will. Call it a shantytown.
Call it a shitshow. The frazzled, dazzled faces
of children left half-dead with hollow eyes.
We were a village once.

In the Abstract

The birds are flying upside down in protest.
The sun is rising in the West and setting over the East.

A vast drama undergoes seismic shifts.
First this arm disappears, then the other.

We were picking oranges in our grove
when we heard it. A racing fighter across the sky.

We proceeded to place the oranges in a basket
the scent so sweet rising to our nostrils.

Next to the farm was a graveyard filled
to the brim with dead soldiers.

My father took me there
on our brown and white mare.

I remember my father's hand strong against her flank.
Guiding her in the sun against shafts of wheat.

I don't know if I knew the word patriotism when I was a child.
I think I more remembered sight and smell.

Patriotism was an abstract concept
my child's mind could not hold.

Eclipse

When the eclipse falls we witness
a total absence of light.

Thoughts recede into the atmosphere
entire populations gone.

Who you once knew as brother
is brother to you no more.

Mothers weep for lost children
as children weep for lost dolls.

The struggle to maintain
one's composure gives way.

Tables lose their legs and sound
its meaning beneath the drone
and whistle of rocket flares.

Now the tempestuous sea rises
in response to missing stars.
All is total darkness.

Waves crest and crackle
on the shore.

Chalk scrawls
of alphabets and hopscotch games
exchanged for missing hands and legs.

The only rocks thrown are those thrown
in anger and utter hopelessness.

Even the grandmothers no longer
recline in rocking chairs, but crawl
down the steps of their own homes.

You can taste the bullets between
their teeth as if they were your own.

Supersonic jets blink madness
across the sky, a sky that loses
its meaning with each succeeding day.

No searchlights can find the missing.
No armies to retrieve the dead.

Only lack of a God who once
cared so deeply for this land.

The Cave

In the cave two children sat.
A boy and a girl, hiding from
the bombings.

What they saw made little sense.
They lived from one day
to the next

with what little food they
had, what little water.

The love they felt for each
other was a wounded ocean.

She made a necklace for him
out of dandelions. He held her
when she cried.

Thus they ruled their quiet kingdom
far from the madness of the village.

They lived there for forty days
and forty nights.

In that time
it rained and the winds were
heavy, and the sky was filled with explosions.

One day the sun appeared and
the ground was heavenly silent.

They were hungry. They hadn't
eaten in some time.

All was emptiness. No bombs,
the killing machines were gone.

They walked down to the village
but all had been engulfed in flames.

Nothing left but charred roofs,
charred walls and smoke rising.

Bodies burned up in postures
of frozen horror.

Their mothers and fathers gone.
Families and neighbors,
the entire village. Gone.

They picked up what they could find.
Some food, a Teddy bear with a missing ear,

wrapped everything up
in a small bag and carried it with them,
searching out the next village.

Odysseus's Return

Our lives are shattered vessels realigned
and glued back together by expert hands.
Museum pieces with a rich history.

Love them or hate them
they are here and have written
their names a thousand times

with each succeeding generation.
Mold them into hearts and you have
the beating of a people.

Gold and silver, olive trees—
two doves on a ledge perched side
by side with the sea behind them.

How we long for freedom
but it seems there's always
a price to pay.

It is written that a hero's return
will be viewed as a villain's
by his enemy.

Each side bearing a legitimate claim
the only solution is to continue the slaughter.
Take sides if you must, your empires are to blame.

Can you forgive us for longing
to see them topple? Always with one
gone, there's another to replace it.

All I ever wanted was to recline in a café
and play chess with an old friend
conveying the latest gossip.

Maybe that was too much
to ask for, to make the memory
of these numbers disappear.

A Letter to My Enemy

What if I told you
that you were right,
that we are, after all

brothers and sisters
living under
the same moon.

We keep banging our heads
against the wall only to come
out bruised and bloodied.

We may not like what lies
outside. The garden we once
tended is overgrown with weeds.

It will take a long time to rebuild.
To plant the seeds, give them
water and watch them grow.

It's backbreaking work,
the sweat and toil that
God has ordained us.

Hard work is good work—
it's what we were
meant to do.

The door is right before us.
Here is the key. Should you
open it, or should I?

In the Depths of Us

Somewhere there's a language
we can speak, deep in the depths
of us.

Somewhere a heart beats
out the words for those who take
the time to listen.

Layers of anger stripped away
to reveal a vulnerable child
who cries in silent pain.

How many sisters must be driven
to the brink of sanity, how many brothers
to build a savage mound of death?

When we're still, the world
moves with us. There's no call
for the prophets to foretell dark tomorrows.

There's only so much we need, and it isn't much.
A little water a little food, the smell of snow
the taste of apricots.

We could feel our way through this darkness,
I know we can—if we only stretch out our fingers
to touch the touch that soothes.

Today is filled with promise—
tomorrow may be gray.
It lives inside us, this gift of breath

that banishes evil thoughts
and lets our actions lead the way.

Miles Liss spent his formative years in Israel, on Moshav Avichael. He experienced the Yom Kippur War in 1973 when he was just a child. Soon after, his family moved back to America and settled in Miami Beach, Florida. The events of October 7th affected him deeply, causing him to reflect on his past and his cultural identity. October 7th and its aftermath also deepened his concern for the future of the Middle East.

Miles has studied poetry at Bread Loaf Writers' Conference and the Colrain Poetry Manuscript Conference, has been awarded a Tupelo Press/MASS MoCA residency, and has attended The Porches Writing Retreat in Linwood, Virginia. He's the winner of the 2021 AWP Kurt Brown Prize in Poetry and was selected as a scholar for the 2024 Yetzirah Jewish Poetry Conference. A collection of original poetry and art, *Some Inconvenient Poems*, is available through Death of Workers Whilst Building Skyscrapers Press. Miles holds an MFA in Writing from Vermont College of Fine Arts.